STICKER ATLAS
My World

Welcome to your world, the Earth.

This sticker atlas contains lots of maps showing the continents, countries, and oceans of our home planet.

Use your stickers to add in the animals, people, and landmarks that make Earth so special and interesting. T̶̶̶ ̶̶̶ facts to read and pl̶̶̶ ̶̶̶ plus a quiz at the e̶̶̶ ̶̶̶ your global knowledge!

T0204576

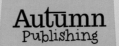

Autumn
Publishing

The World

It is very cold north of the Arctic Circle, with a large part of the Arctic Ocean covered by ice.

Arctic Ocean

The Arctic

ARCTIC CIRCLE

NORTH AMERICA

Atlantic Ocean

TROPIC OF CANCER

Central America

EQUATOR

The Equator, as shown on maps by a line, runs around the middle of the world.

TROPIC OF CAPRICORN

SOUTH AMERICA

When it is summer south of the Tropic of Capricorn, it is winter north of the Tropic of Cancer, and vice versa.

Antarctica is the coldest place on our planet.

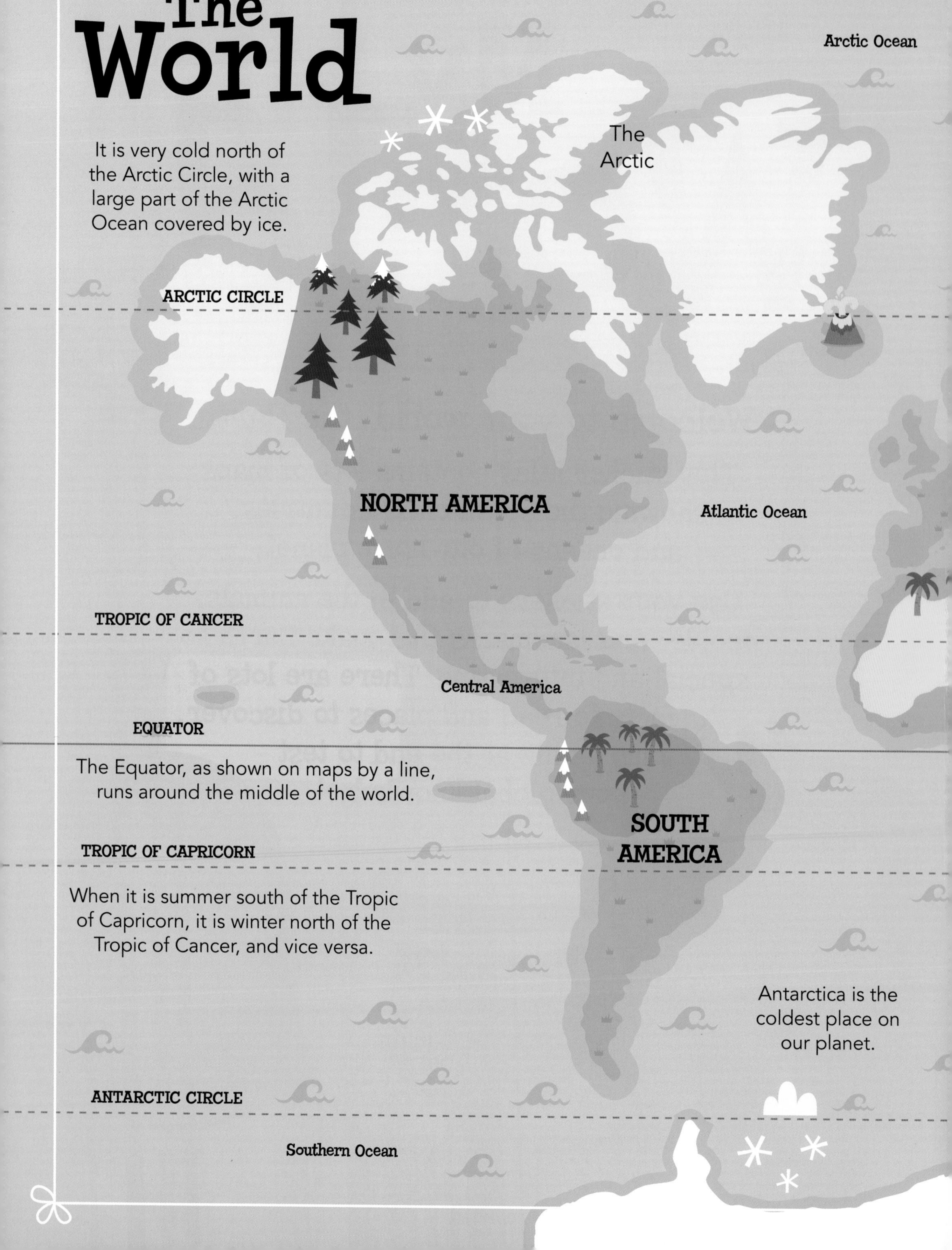

ANTARCTIC CIRCLE

Southern Ocean

On Earth there are over 190 countries, spread across seven large areas of land called continents, separated by five oceans. From the tall mountains to the deep oceans, there's lots to discover!

EUROPE

ASIA

Pacific Ocean

The lands between the Tropics of Cancer and Capricorn are known as the 'Tropics.'

AFRICA

Indian Ocean

AUSTRALIA AND OCEANIA

Antarctica is the only continent that doesn't border another continent.

True north always points to the North Pole in the Arctic.

ANTARCTICA

Africa

Africa is the world's second largest and second most populated continent. It is surrounded by three seas and three oceans. Africa is home to one billion people living in a land of deserts, rainforests, mountains, and savannahs.

The largest country in Africa is Algeria. The smallest is the Seychelles, an island 1,135 miles north of Madagascar.

North Africa is home to the Sahara Desert. It is as large as the USA!

The River Nile is the longest river in the world, at 4,258 miles.

Mediterranean Sea

Red Sea

Arabian Sea

River Nile

Pyramids of Giza

Atlas Mountains

Sahara Desert

Dromedary camel

River Niger

Zuma Rock

Sudanese man

MADEIRA (PORTUGAL)

CANARY ISLANDS (SPAIN)

WESTERN SAHARA

MOROCCO

TUNISIA

ALGERIA

LIBYA

EGYPT

MAURITANIA

MALI

NIGER

CHAD

SUDAN

ERITREA

DJIBOUTI

ETHIOPIA

SENEGAL

THE GAMBIA

GUINEA-BISSAU

GUINEA

SIERRA LEONE

LIBERIA

CÔTE D'IVOIRE

GHANA

TOGO

BENIN

BURKINA FASO

NIGERIA

CAMEROON

CENTRAL AFRICAN REPUBLIC

SOUTH SUDAN

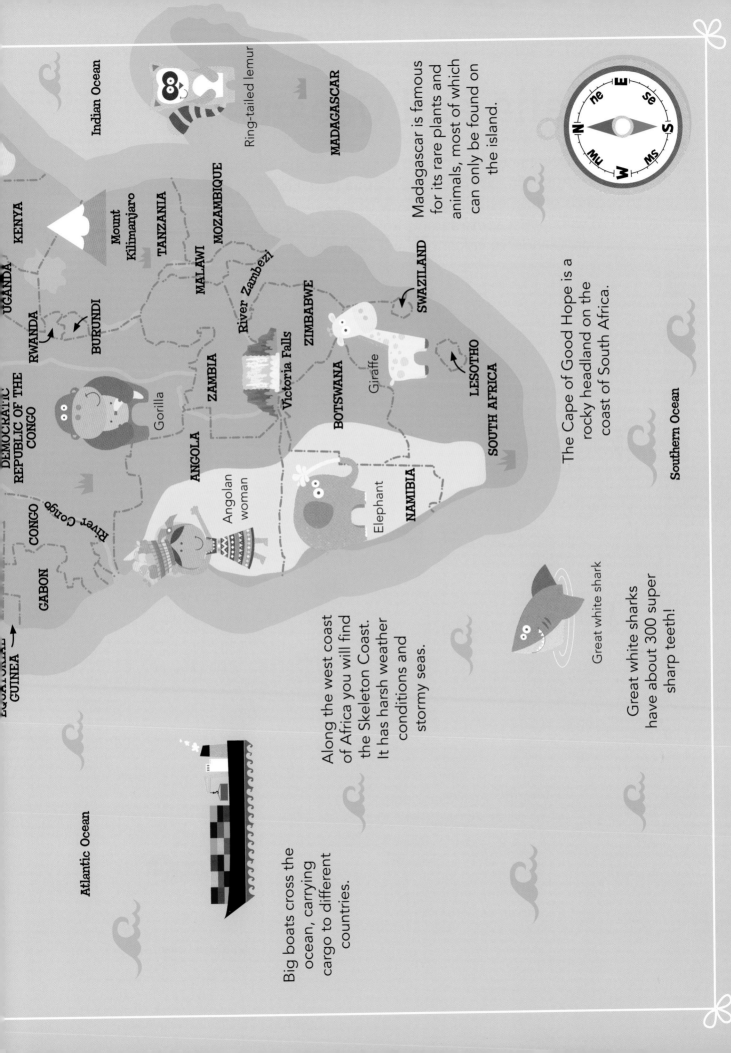

Indian Ocean

Ring-tailed lemur

MADAGASCAR

Madagascar is famous for its rare plants and animals, most of which can only be found on the island.

KENYA
UGANDA

Mount Kilimanjaro

TANZANIA

RWANDA
BURUNDI

MALAWI

MOZAMBIQUE

River Zambezi

SWAZILAND

ZIMBABWE

Victoria Falls

Giraffe

BOTSWANA

DEMOCRATIC REPUBLIC OF THE CONGO

Gorilla

ZAMBIA

LESOTHO

SOUTH AFRICA

ANGOLA

The Cape of Good Hope is a rocky headland on the coast of South Africa.

Angolan woman

NAMIBIA

Elephant

Southern Ocean

CONGO

River Congo

GABON

EQUATORIAL GUINEA

Great white shark

Great white sharks have about 300 super sharp teeth!

Atlantic Ocean

Big boats cross the ocean, carrying cargo to different countries.

Along the west coast of Africa you will find the Skeleton Coast. It has harsh weather conditions and stormy seas.

Australia and Oceania

Australia and Oceania is the smallest continent in the world, made up of Australia, New Zealand, Papua New Guinea, and thousands of tropical islands. Many of these islands are uninhabited with landscapes ranging from rainforests and dry grasslands, to volcanoes and deserts.

Scuba diver

CHRISTMAS ISLAND

Red crab

Indian Ocean

Red crabs live in the forests of Christmas Island but migrate every year to the sea to lay eggs.

Kangaroo

AUSTRALIA

Uluru (Ayers Rock)

Ranger with boomerang

Bottlenose dolphin

Native Australians are called Aborigines. They have a rich culture from music and art to myths and legends. Aboriginal mythology is known as 'Dreamtime.'

Surfer

Southern Ocean

NAURU

The largest country
in Australia and Oceania
is Australia. The smallest is
the island nation of Nauru,
near Papua New Guinea.

SOLOMON
ISLANDS

TUVALU

PAPUA NEW
GUINEA

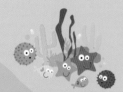

VANUATU

FIJI

Hunga
Tonga
underwater
volcano

The Great
Barrier Reef

NEW
CALEDONIA
(FRANCE)

In 2015, a new island was
created when Hunga Tonga
erupted. The island hasn't
been named as it may soon
disappear.

Darling River

Koala

TONGA

Murray River

Pacific Ocean

Maori man

Many animals and plants
are native to Australia and
Oceania. This means they
can't be found anywhere else
in the world! These include
the koala, kangaroo, and
Tasmanian devil.

NEW ZEALAND

TASMANIA
(AUSTRALIA)

New
Zealand
lambs

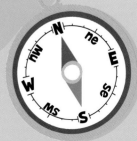

North America

Arctic Ocean

Walrus

Dog sledding

Moose

Great Bear Lake

ALASKA (USA)

Great Slave Lake

Rocky Mountains

CANADA

Bald eagle

Ice hockey player

Gulf of Alaska

110 years ago, blue whales were almost extinct in this part of the world. Now there are over 2,200 blue whales living in the ocean between Mexico and Alaska.

Offshore oil rig

Missouri River

UNITED STATES OF AMERICA

Blue whale

Pacific Ocean

Hollywood

Man wearing a serape

The largest country in North America is Canada, and the smallest is Saint Kitts and Nevis, a two-island nation in the Caribbean.

Hawaii is part of the United States of America. It is the only state with a rainforest and a royal palace!

MEXICO

Hula dancer

HAWAII (USA)

North America is the third largest continent and consists of 23 countries, including America, Canada, Greenland, and Mexico. It is the only continent that has every type of climate, including the freezing cold temperatures of Greenland, the dry deserts of Nevada, and the tropical rainforests of Costa Rica.

GREENLAND (DENMARK)

Labrador Sea

Hudson Bay

North American beaver

Although it is within the area of the North American continent, Greenland is actually part of Denmark in Europe. About 81% of Greenland is covered by a sheet of ice. All the cities are on the coastline, where there is no ice.

Great Lakes

Green sea turtle

Niagara Falls

Atlantic Ocean

Mississippi River

The Statue of Liberty

Football player

Central America is a 'land bridge' (or isthmus) between North and South America, but is part of the continent of North America.

Gulf of Mexico

THE BAHAMAS

CUBA

DOMINICAN REPUBLIC

HAITI

Pyramid of Chichén Itzá

BELIZE

JAMAICA

PUERTO RICO (USA)

UATEMALA

L SALVADOR

HONDURAS

Caribbean Sea

NICARAGUA

COSTA RICA

PANAMA

South America

South America, the fourth largest continent, is home to the world's highest waterfall (Angel Falls), the largest river (the Amazon River), the longest mountain range (the Andes), the driest place on Earth (the Atacama Desert), the largest rainforest (the Amazon Rainforest), and the highest capital city (La Paz in Bolivia).

The largest country in South America is Brazil, the smallest country is Suriname.

VENEZUELA

COLOMBIA

GUYANA

SURINAME

FRENCH GUIANA

ECUADOR

PERU

BRAZIL

BOLIVIA

PARAGUAY

GALAPAGOS

Angel Falls

Toucan

Amazon River

Piranha

Jaguar

Machu Picchu

Giant tortoise

Carnival dancer

Christ the Redeemer

Soccer player

60% of the Amazon Rainforest is in Brazil.

Lonesome George was the last giant Pinta Island tortoise in the world. He died in 2012 at 100 years old.

Atlantic Ocean

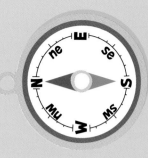

Angler fish

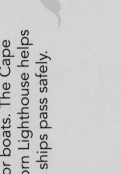

Uruguay River

URUGUAY

ARGENTINA

Argentinian gaucho

Atacama Desert

Boa constrictor

The Magellan Strait is where Atlantic and Pacific waters mix, making it dangerous for boats. The Cape Horn Lighthouse helps ships pass safely.

Cape Horn Lighthouse

Andean condor

The Andes Mountains

CHILE

Pacific Ocean

The Andes Mountains pass through seven countries and are home to more than 600 mammal species, including llamas, chinchillas, and cougars.

Octopus

West Europe

Europe is the second smallest continent but is the third most populated. The climate in western Europe ranges greatly, from the cold temperatures of northern parts of Norway and Sweden to the mediterranean warmth found in the south of France, Spain, Italy, and Greece.

Vikings settled on the Faroe Islands in the 9th Century, and their descendents are still living there today!

ICELAND

Atlantic Ocean

Atlantic cod

FAROE ISLANDS (DENMARK)

Lifeboat

Kayaker

NORWAY

Puffin

SWEDEN

Dala horse

DENMARK

Moose

FINLAND

Baltic Sea

LATVIA

N
ne
E
se
S
sw
W
nw

East Europe

The east of Europe contains part of Russia (which makes up 38% of Europe's land mass), the Baltic states of Lithuania, Latvia, and Estonia, and eastern European countries including Romania and Bulgaria. The east of Europe connects to Asia, with parts of Russia and Turkey spanning two continents.

Ural Mountains

Ballet dancer

Russia is the largest country in Europe, and in the world, covering over 10% of the Earth's surface.

RUSSIA

Arctic Ocean

Wild boar

Volga-Baltic Waterway

POST OFFICE

Santa Claus's Main Post Office

Santa Claus's Main Post Office receives 550,000 letters each year from all over the world. Over 100,000 of these letters are from children in the United Kingdom.

FINLAND

Baltic Sea

Golden eagle

The Volga River is the longest river in Europe, with a length of over 2,200 miles.

The Caspian Sea is the world's largest inland body of water.

Volga River

Caspian Sea

Caucasian Mountains

St Basil's Cathedral

East Caucasian tur

Dnieper River

Black Sea

Cossack dancer

ESTONIA

LATVIA

LITHUANIA

Common European adder

BELARUS

UKRAINE

MOLDOVA

Bran Castle in Romania is said to have links to Count Dracula.

ROMANIA

Bran Castle

BULGARIA

TURKEY

West Asia

Asia is the largest continent on Earth. The west of Asia is separated from Europe by the Ural Mountains, which run from the north of Russia to northwestern Kazakhstan. There is a contrast in climate between dry, rainless deserts and moist forests covering the mountains.

Fabergé eggs

Fabergé eggs are beautifully decorated ornaments that were originally given as gifts at Easter. The first Fabergé egg was given to the empress of Russia.

Ob River

Woman in sarafan dress

Wild horse

The largest country in Asia is Russia, which spans Europe and Asia. The smallest country is the Maldives.

Matryoshka dolls

Eurasian wolf

RUSSIA

The National Space Agency

The forests of the Ural Mountains are home to animals including the brown bear, lynx, wolverine, and elk.

Volga River

Ural Mountains

Don River

Dnieper River

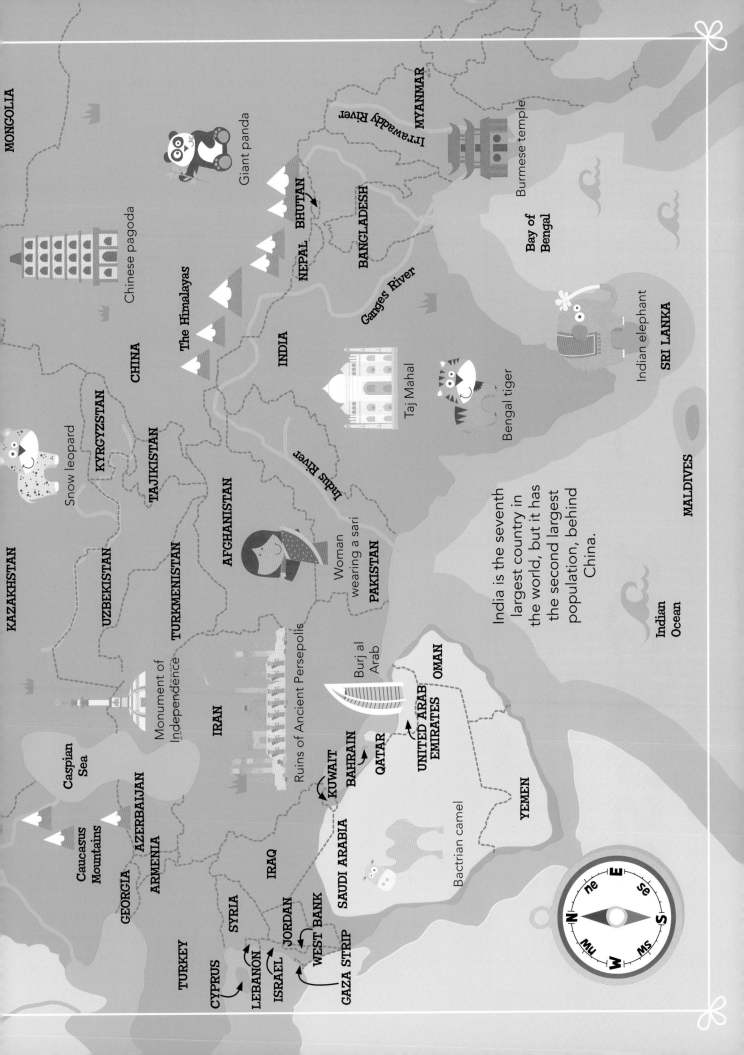

MONGOLIA

Giant panda

Chinese pagoda

MYANMAR

Irrawaddy River

Burmese temple

BHUTAN

NEPAL

BANGLADESH

The Himalayas

Ganges River

Bay of
Bengal

CHINA

KYRGYZSTAN

TAJIKISTAN

INDIA

Taj Mahal

Bengal tiger

Indian elephant

SRI LANKA

Snow leopard

KAZAKHSTAN

UZBEKISTAN

AFGHANISTAN

Indus River

Woman
wearing a sari

PAKISTAN

MALDIVES

TURKMENISTAN

Monument of
Independence

India is the seventh
largest country in
the world, but it has
the second largest
population, behind
China.

Indian
Ocean

Caspian
Sea

IRAN

Ruins of Ancient Persepolis

Burj al
Arab

OMAN

AZERBAIJAN

Caucasus
Mountains

ARMENIA

GEORGIA

IRAQ

KUWAIT

BAHRAIN

QATAR

UNITED ARAB
EMIRATES

TURKEY

CYPRUS

SYRIA

LEBANON

ISRAEL

JORDAN

WEST BANK

GAZA STRIP

SAUDI ARABIA

YEMEN

Bactrian camel

N
ne
E
se
S
sw
W
nw

East Asia

As well as being the largest continent, Asia also has the largest population. 60% of the world's population lives in Asia. Many of the islands in Asia were created by ancient underwater volcanoes. Some of these islands are still growing due to volcanic activity.

A journey on the Trans-Siberian Railway can take you all the way from Moscow to the Great Wall of China, passing through Siberia, Mongolia, the Gobi Desert, and Beijing.

Siberia is a vast, cold area of Russia's central and eastern regions. It is so cold that some of the land is covered in permafrost, which is frozen soil that never thaws.

Brown bears

Russia has the largest population of brown bears in the world, with over 100,000 living in the mountains and forests.

Lena River

Siberian tiger

Yenisei River

RUSSIA

Lake Baikal

The Great Wall of China is just under 5,500 miles long. When it was originally built it was over 13,000 miles, which is over half the length of the equator!

Valley of Geysers

Trans-Siberian Railway

MONGOLIA

Mongolian yurt

10. Name the largest rainforest in the world.

11. What is the smallest country in Europe, and the world?

12. Where is Santa Claus's Main Post Office?

a. The North Pole   b. Finland   c. The Arctic

13. Which country has the largest population?

14. Name the biggest country in the world.

15. What would you find at the North Pole?

a. A pole   b. A thick layer of ice   c. A colony of penguins

16. What three words could you use to describe the weather in Antarctica?

ANSWERS

1. Asia, Africa, North America, South America, Antarctica, Europe, and Australia and Oceania.
2. Arctic Ocean, Pacific Ocean, Atlantic Ocean, Southern Ocean, and Indian Ocean.
3. a. Skeleton Coast. 4. The River Nile in Egypt. 5. a. Australia and Oceania.
6. E.g. Koala, kangaroo, and Tasmanian Devil. 7. Hawaii! 8. b. North America. 9. c. Venezuela.
10. The Amazon Rainforest. 11. Vatican City. 12. b. Finland. 13. China. 14. Russia.
15. b. A thick layer of ice. 16. Dry, cold, and windy.

World records

The world is full of things that are...

big and small

long and short

high and low

Can you spot where the places in **bold** below are on the maps?

★ The biggest country in the world is **Russia**. The smallest country is **Vatican City**.

★ The highest natural point on Earth is **Mount Everest** in Asia.

★ The lowest natural point on Earth is Challenger Deep, at the bottom of the **Mariana Trench** in the Pacific Ocean.

★ The longest river is **The Nile** in North Africa. The shortest river is Roe River in America.

★ The coldest temperature measured on Earth was in **Antarctica** (-143.32 degrees Fahrenheit). The warmest temperature measured on Earth was in Death Valley in the USA (134.06 degrees Fahrenheit).

★ The most densely populated country in the world is **Monaco**. The least densely populated country in the world is **Greenland**.

★ The country with the most neighbors is **China**. There are 14 countries bordering it. See if you can count all of them!

★ There are only three countries in the world that are surrounded entirely by one other country. These are: **Lesotho** surrounded by South Africa, **San Marino** surrounded by Italy, and **Vatican City** surrounded by the city of Rome in Italy.

 Sudanese man

 Pyramids of Giza

 Lion

 Gorilla

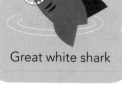 Elephant

 Giraffe

 Dromedary camel

 Ring-tailed lemur

 Angolan woman

 Great white shark

 Red crab

 Kangaroo

 Bottlenose dolphin

 Maori man

 New Zealand lambs

 Ranger with boomerang

 Surfer

 Dog sledding

 Koala

 Scuba diver

 Offshore oil rig

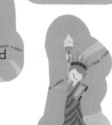 Hollywood

 Bald eagle

 Ice hockey player

 Moose

 Man wearing a serape

 The Statue of Liberty

Pyramid of Chichén Itzá

 Blue whale

Walrus

 North American beaver

Hula dancer

Carnival dancer

Piranha

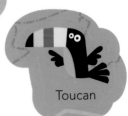
Green sea turtle

Football player

Soccer player

Christ the Redeemer

Argentinian gaucho

Toucan

Andean condor

Machu Picchu

Jaguar

Boa Constrictor

Angler fish

Giant tortoise

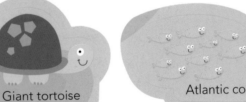
Atlantic cod

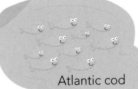
Big Ben

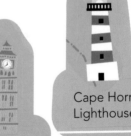
Cape Horn Lighthouse

Octopus

Dala horse

Irish dancer

Lifeboat

Flamenco dancer

The Eiffel Tower

Moose

Kayaker

Jet skier

Puffin

 Neuschwanstein Castle

 Dutch girl

 White stork

 The Parthenon

 The Leaning Tower of Pisa

 Santa Claus's Main Post Office

 St Basil's Cathedral

 Golden eagle

 Ballet dancer

 Wild boar

 Common European adder

 East Caucasian tur

 The National Space Agency

 Bran Castle

 Cossack dancer

 Matryoshka dolls

 Fabergé eggs

 Eurasian wolf

 Bengal tiger

 Snow leopard

 Woman in sarafan dress

 Wild horse

 Taj Mahal

 Chinese pagoda

 Monument of Independence

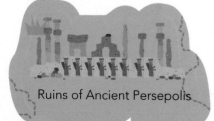 Ruins of Ancient Persepolis

 Bactrian camel

 Woman wearing a sari

 Giant panda